# Too Much Soap

Written by Jan Burchett and Sara Vogler
Illustrated by Anastasiya Kanavaliuk

**Collins**

I get lots of soap.

The room is full of foam.

Up I go on a carpet of foam!

I am high up in the dark night air.

I can see a road in the moonlight.

I see car lights.

Look! A barn owl.

Wow! I shoot higher than the rooftops.

# Can I shoot to the moon?

No! The soap is popping!

I am sinking. Down, down, down.

# That was fantastic!

13

# Soap

#  Review: After reading

Use your assessment from hearing the children read to choose any GPCs, words or tricky words that need additional practice.

## Read 1: Decoding

- On page 4, discuss the meaning of **carpet**.
  - Ask: In what ways could foam be like a **carpet**? (e.g. *it's a layer to sit on*)
- Ask the children to read the words and find the matching pairs that contain the same sounds, spelled with two letters. Ask: Which is the odd one out? (*look – because of its short /**oo**/ sound*)

  | | | | |
  |---|---|---|---|
  | **foam** | **dark** | **roof** | **car** |
  | **look** | **shoot** | **road** | |

- Encourage the children to read these words, blending the words in their heads first, before sounding them out.

  | | | |
  |---|---|---|
  | **carpet** | **rooftops** | **fantastic** |
  | **moonlight** | **higher** | |

## Read 2: Prosody

- Turn to pages 10 and 11 and focus on the punctuation.
  - On page 10, point out the question mark and encourage the children to try emphasising different words so it sounds like a thoughtful question.
  - On page 11, point out the exclamation marks. Discuss how the boy is feeling. (e.g. *surprised, disappointed, worried*) Ask the children to read the words with emotion.
  - Ask the children to read both pages, emphasising the change of tone.

## Read 3: Comprehension

- Ask the children if they have played with soapy foam. Ask: What did the foam look and feel like?
- Ask: What is this story about? Does the boy really go up on a carpet of foam?
  - Discuss the ways in which it is a story about an imaginary magic carpet. Refer to stories the children may already know about flying carpets.
  - Return to pages 11 and 12. Ask: What brought the journey to an end? (*the bubbles in the foam popped*)
- Ask the children to retell what happened on the boy's journey using pages 14 and 15.
- Ask the children to suggest what might happen next time the boy goes up on a carpet of foam.
  - Where might he go and what might he see?
  - What will make him come down again?